HARDPRESS.NET
HOME OF HARD-TO-FIND BOOKS

Memoirs of the Count of Comminge
by Claudine Alexandrine Guérin De Tencin

1. Fiction, Fee

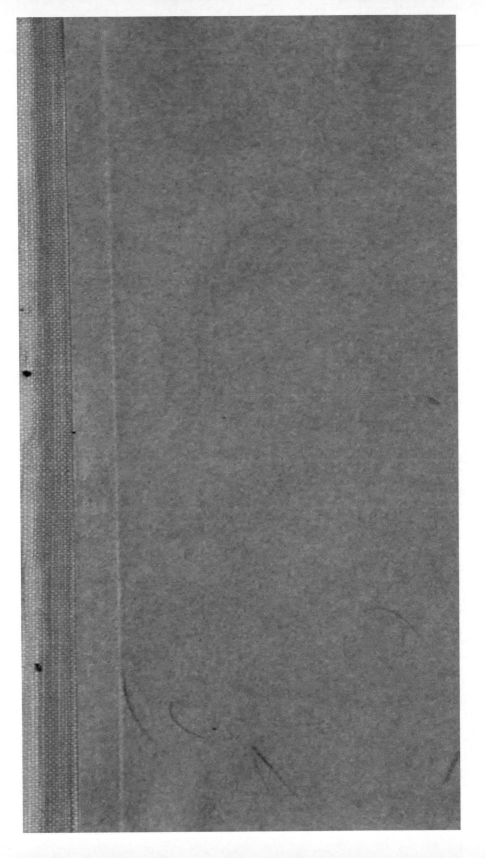

suild-

MEMOIRS

OF THE

COUNT OF COMMINGE.

From the FRENCH

OF

MONSIEUR D'ARNAUD.

Qui pungit cor, profert fensum.
Ecclesiast. C. 22. V. 19.

LONDON:

Printed for G. KEARSLY, at No. 46, opposite
Fetter Lane, Fleet-Street, 1774.

A
SKETCH

OF THE

ABBEY OF LA TRAPPE.

THE Abbey of la Trappe is
situated in an extensive vale on
the borders of Perche and Normandy,
which seems designed by nature the
retreat of penitence ; it being environ-
ed with woods, lakes, and mountains,
which render it almost inaccessible.

In this solitude silence ever reigns :
language can but faintly paint the
melancholy scene ; a scene teeming
with the most noble traits for the
gloomy imagination of a painter or
a poet.

The

The venerable groves which caſt the cypreſs gloom, the winds whiſtling through the foliage which superſtition conſtrues inauſpicious, the dying murmurs of the waters which gurgle over the pebbles, announce the confines of la Trappe.

It was founded by Rotrou, count du Perche, in the year 1140, to accompliſh a vow made in the perils of ſhipwreck ; and it aſſumed the name of la *Trappe*, from the *ſtairs* which lead down to it.

Perpetual ſilence is the grand rule impoſed on the recluſe of this convent. It is the very eſſence of the inſtitution ; and it was deemed a matter

of

of fuch high import in the founder's eye, that he intimated to thofe pious anchorites, that breaking filence would be to them a crime of not lefs heinous die than blafphemy itfelf. The language of the convent therefore confifts rather in figns than words: and if neceffity provokes one of the order at any time to violate this rigid prohibition, he muft fpeak in a whifper with all poffible concifenefs.——

Society has no fweets for thefe holy men; they being debarred not only the pleafures arifing from rational converfation, but are abfolutely fecluded from communicating their thoughts in writing.

Their

Their diet is of the coarfeft viands, and diftributed with a fparing hand.

A plank covered with ftraw, is all the luxury of their dormitory.

Few hours are allowed for refrefh-ment; they being fummoned to ma-tins at two in the morning, which continue till the day calls them to difcharge the menial fervices of the convent; in which the aged and the infirm are indifcriminately employed.

Medicine is unknown within thefe walls; the fick are ftrangers to every indulgence; they rife up early, and late take reft. They muft fpend the day in prayer and in labour propor-tionate

tionate to their ſtrength : they hear not the ſoothing voice of conſolation, they feel not the alleviating hand of friendſhip, but muſt drink the cup of bitterneſs in all its horrors. They perſevere in ſilence, abſtinence, and mortification, till the hour of death approaches ; then they are ſupported to the chapel, receive the extreme unction, and are ſtretched on a plank ſtrewed with aſhes : in this comfortleſs ſituation they wait the moment of departure with tranquillity, with cheerfulneſs, with joy ; and exhibit prodigies of heroiſm known only to theſe chriſtian philoſophers.——

I T was thought neceſſary, for the better underſtanding the following hiſtory, to give the above outlines of the inſtitution and ſituation of la Trappe; and for the gratification of thoſe minds which are diſſatisfied with fictitious ſcenes of miſery, to premiſe that the moſt ſtriking incidents in the ſubſequent Memoirs, have been un-happily realized.

MEMOIRS

OF THE

COUNT OF COMMINGE.

MY fole motive for writing thefe memoirs is to recal the minuteft circumftances of my misfortunes, and engrave them, if poffible, more deeply on my memory.

I am defcended from the houfe of Comminge, one of the moft illuftrious families in the kingdom. My great-

B   grand-

grand-father, who had two children, made the youngeft his heir in prejudice to his brother, and ordered him to affume the name and title of Marquis of Luffan. The partiality of the parent abated not the affection of the children, who were equally defirous, that their fons fhould be educated together, that the force of blood might be more clofely united in the tender bands of friendfhip; but their wifhes were ineffectual, and their utmoft endeavours proved abortive; for the children imbibed an enmity in their cradles, which terminated only with their lives.

My

My father, who was greatly inferior in abilities to the young Marquis, conceived an antipathy to him, which time improved into the most inveterate hatred. They had perpetual quarrels, and as my father was ever the aggressor, he alone was punished. At length he complained to the steward of our family, who told him he could furnish him with the means to humble the pride of the Marquis : for, added he, the Marquis's estate is entailed on you, and your grand-father had no power to dispose of it ; after your father's decease therefore it will not be difficult to recover your right.

This

This converfation eftranged my father entirely from his coufin; and their mutual animofities were carried to fuch excefs, that a feparation was the unavoidable confequence. They faw not each other for many years, during which period they both were married; the Marquis of Luffan had a daughter, an only child; my father had none but me.

As foon as the death of my grandfather had put him in poffeffion of his eftate, my father practifed the fteward's advice. He fearched after proofs to confirm his title, he rejected every propofal of accommodation, and entered

tered a procefs againft the Marquis; which in the end could not fail ftripping him of his whole eftate. An unfortunate rencounter in hunting rendered them irreconcilable; my father, ever haughty and malicious, infulted the Marquis on the condition to which he fhould reduce him, in terms the moft opprobrious: the Marquis, tho' naturally of an eafy temper, could not forbear reply; this altercation brought on a duel, which terminated in favour of the Marquis, who difarmed my father and bid him beg his life. Even life, fays he, would be odious, if to you I owed it. To me you fhall owe it, replied the Marquis;

B 3 and

and toffing him his fword, he left him.

This generous act affected not my father; his prejudices on the contrary were encreafed by the double victory his enemy had gained over him; and he profecuted with implacable affiduity, the fuit he had commenced againft him.

Things were thus circumftanced when I returned from my travels. I had been in the country but few days, when the Abbot of Rouillon (a relation of my mother's) acquainted us, that the titles of the eftate, on which

depended

depended the fuccefs of the law-fuit, were lodged in the archives of his abbey, where the title-deeds of our own family had been concealed during the confufion of the civil wars. This information my father was moft carefully to conceal, and to fearch in perfon for the papers, or fend one in whom he could repofe the moft implicit confidence. As my father was in an ill ftate of health, he charged me with the commiffion, having previoufly exaggerated the importance of it. The fuccefs of your refearches, fays he, will tend more to your emolument than mine, fince on recovering the eftate, I will immediately veft

it

it in you : but exclufive of your own intereft, I flatter myfelf you fo fenfibly feel the wrongs of your father, that you will moft cordially affift him in revenging the injuries he has received.

I had no reafon to refufe my father's requeft, therefore affured him of my obedience; and having received all neceffary inftructions, it was thought expedient for me to affume the name and title of Marquis of Longville, the better to efcape fufpicion in the abbey, where the Marchionefs of Luffan had many relations. An old domeftic of my father's, and my own valet de chambre

chambre were my sole attendants. I
hastened to the abbey, where I found
the title deeds, which incontestably
confirmed the entail, and acquainted
my father with it, begging permission
at the same time to spend some days
at the Wells which were in the neighbourhood. The success of my re-
searches bribed my father to consent,
and I set out to the Wells immediately,
retaining my feigned name, as it
would have been requisite to have appeared with a grander retinue to support the dignity of the House of
Comminge.

The

The day after my arrival I was introduced to the company, and as in thofe places of public refort the ftiffnefs of ceremonial gives way to freedom of behaviour, I was immediately admitted into all the parties of pleafure.

I dined with the Marquis of Valette, who gave an elegant entertainment to the ladies, moft of whom I had feen before at the Wells, and had paid them fome general compliments, agreeable to the gallantry of the age. To thefe ladies I was talking indifcriminately, when a matron of moft noble prefence entered the room, attended

tended by her daughter, who was
bleffed with the moft perfect fymme-
try of features, and elegance of perfon ; her unaffuming modefty heightened the glow of youth, and added
grace to every charm. I loved in-
ftantaneoufly, and the firft moment
decided my fate. My gaiety vanifhed,
and my whole attention was folely
fixed on her. She perceived my anxiety with a blufh. A walk was pro-
pofed, and I had the happinefs to
give my hand to the moft lovely of
her fex. We were at fuch diftance
from the company, that I had a fair
opportunity of difclofing the fentiments of my heart ; but I, who had

3   my

my eyes rivetted on her before without ceasing, could not now, when unobserved, dare raise them from the earth. In my gallantry with the fair, my heart had hitherto been a stranger to the dictates of my tongue; but now I could not conceal from myself the tender emotions with which I was moved.

We rejoined the company without having opened my lips; the ladies retired to their respective houses, and I to my lodgings, the better to enjoy my anxiety, which was blended with a gleam of joy, a joy that ever accompanies the commencement of love.

My

My passion had rendered me so timid that I dared not even enquire the name of my beloved, as if my curiosity would have betrayed the sentiments of my soul. But what was my situation, when I heard the lady was daughter to the Marquis of Lussan!

Every thing I had to apprehend from the enmity of our families flashed upon my memory. But of all the melancholy reflections, which presented themselves to view, the dread of Adelaid's being inspired with aversion to every one of our family, was by far the most intolerable. I could not but applaud myself for having assumed

affumed a feigned name, and flattered
myfelf, that under this difguife I fhould
make her confcious of my love without prepoffefling her againft me; and
that when at length I fhould difcover
the deceit, I fhould excite at leaft her
pity.

I was determined more ftudioufly to
conceal my name, and to exert every
talent which might render me agreeable. I haunted Adelaid as her
fhadow; my fole wifh was to have
an opportunity of fpeaking to her
alone, which when it offered, I dared
not take: the fear of lofing a thoufand little liberties, and much more

the

the apprehenfion of her difpleafure, frightened me into filence.

In this ftate of inquietude I had lived for fome time ; at length a fine evening enticed the company to walk, when Adelaid accidentally dropped her braceler, in which was fet her picture. The Chevalier de St. Odon very officioufly picked it up ; and having attentively furveyed it, with great compofure depofited it in his pocket. She begged him to return it with much good humour, but on his refufal fpoke with fome warmth.

The

The Chevalier was a man of addrefs, but his fuccefs with the fair had made him vain and coxcomical. Adelaid's peremptory demand nothing difconcerted him ; he afked her with a fmile, whether fhe would deprive him of that for which he was indebted to chance alone.

I flatter myfelf, added he, in a lower tone of voice, that when you are acquainted with my fentiments, you will have no objection to my keeping what fortune has thus gracioufly thrown in my way, and without waiting for an anfwer, inftantly withdrew.

I was

I was at fome fmall diftance, during this fracas, with the Marchionefs of Valette; but when I perceived that the voice of Adelaid was more than ufually animated, I drew near, but failed not in thofe attentions which refpect requires. She related the circumftance to her mother with fome emotion. The Marchionefs was not lefs angry than her daughter. I fpoke not a word, but continued my walk with the ladies, and having waited on them home, I then immediately went in fearch of the Chevalier. I found him at home, told him the purport of my vifit, and that I fhould wait for him at a place appòinted. He

C   accepted

accepted my invitation, and met me accordingly. I am perfuaded, faid I, immediately accofting him, that the affair which happened on the walks was a mere pleafantry, but I am fure you are too gallant a man to keep a lady's picture without her permiffion. I know not, replies he, what intereft you may have in the affair, but this I know, that I never permit advice to be thus impertinently intruded on me. I truft, faid I, laying my hand upon my fword, that this will enforce my advice, and oblige you to follow it.

The Chevalier was brave, and drew immediately ; we fought for fome

time

time with equal addreſs; but he was
not animated with love like mine;
my paſſion threw me off my guard,
and laid me open to two flight wounds;
in return I made a dangerous but ſuc-
ceſsful thruſt, which obliged him to
beg his life and return the picture.
Having raiſed him up and conducted
him to a houſe adjacent, I retired to
my lodgings and dreſſed my wounds.
Then I examined the dear picture,
and imprinted on it a thouſand kiſſes.
In painting I was an adept, and had
now an opportunity of exerting my
ſkill. What cannot love perform! I
copied the picture the ſame night, and
ſo happily ſucceeded, that I myſelf

could

could scarce diftinguifh the copy from
the original. This gave me the idea
of fubftituting the one for the other.
In keeping the original I found a
lover's advantage, that then even without her knowledge, fhe would oblige
me by honouring my work with her
notice ; thefe things are no trifles in the
eye of a lover, as my heart full well can
teftify.——After having difpofed the
bracelet in its former fhape that my
theft might efcape detection, I carried
it to Adelaid. The Marchionefs of
Luffan faid a thoufand obliging things
on the occafion ; Adelaid indeed fpake
but little ; fhe appeared embarraffed ;
but a gleam of joy in being obliged

to

to me, seemed to shine through her confusion, which gave me the most heart-felt satisfaction.

I have in my life experienced some few of those delicious moments, and if my misfortunes had not been uncommonly great, I should not have thought them too dearly purchased.

This litttle adventure was productive of the most favourable consequences; it gained me such intimacy in the family, that I had frequent opportunities of seeing Adelaid: and although I never had disclosed my sentiments, was well assured, they had

not

not efcaped her notice: and I had
fome reafon to imagine that I was not
wholly difagreeable to her. Hearts
fufceptible as ours are not long ftrangers to each other, but moft fenfibly
exprefs the delicate feelings of the
foul.

Two months had glided on in this
amufive manner, when a letter from
my father ordered me to return. This
was like a thunder-bolt too forcible to
be withftood. I had been fo wholly
wrapped up in the pleafing thoughts
of feeing and loving Adelaid, that the
idea of our being feparated was per-
fectly new; My grief on the occafion,

fion, my reflections on the continuation of the law-fuit unhappily fubfifting between our families, with every thing that was odious, prefented themfelves to my view; I paffed the night in mifery inexpreffible, and after project-ing a thoufand fchemes which died away in embryo, it on a fudden ftruck me to deftroy the papers relative to the eftate, which confirmed our title to the domains of the houfe of Luffan. I was aftonifhed that the fcheme had not before engaged my attention, fince it muft infallibly prevent the confequences of that law-fuit, which fo much I feared. I even reproached myfelf for having kept fo

long,

long, what my tendernefs ought much fooner to have deftroyed. The injury I was doing my father feemed of little confequence; as I could transfer to him an eftate, which a relation had bequeathed me, far fuperior to that I was going to deprive him of.

Little is requifite to convince a man in love, I thought I had a right to difpofe of thofe papers; I fearched the cafket which contained them, and never knew a happier moment, than that which gave them to the flames. The idea of obliging my beloved ravifhed my very foul. If fhe loves me, faid I, fhe fhall know the facrifice

I have

I have made; but if I cannot touch her heart, let her ever remain in ignorance. How fhall I endure her regret at being obliged to me? That Adelaid may love me, from my heart I pray, but I wifh not to burden her with obligations. Not her gratitude, but her affection is the fole object of my defires.

I cannot but confefs, that the confcioufnefs of what I had done, imboldened me to fpeak with greater freedom; and as the moment of my departure was at hand, I feized the firft favourable opportunity.

Beautiful

Beautiful Adelaid, said I, the moment approaches, which must separate me from you ; will you deign sometimes to think of the man, whose future happiness depends alone on you ? My grief was too big for utterance, I could speak no more. She answered me not ; but seemed confused and melancholy. Have you, said I, heard me with a favourable ear ? Answer me, for heaven's sake answer me, though but a word ! what would you that I should say ? I ought not to understand you, I ought not to reply.——

She had scarce pronounced these words, when she abruptly left me ; and though I watched every opportunity,

tunity, I could not speak to her the remainder of the day. She studiously avoided me; her air was much confused, and I was apprehensive, that by my assurance, I had forfeited her esteem. I attended on her with reverential silence, and should have continued this behaviour so conformable to my respect, and agreeable to the delicacy of my sentiments, had not the necessity I was under to leave her, urged me to break silence. I wished before my departure to acquaint her with my real name; a confession which gave me more concern than even the declaration of my love. O my Adelaid, why do you so carefully avoid me!

me ! what then will you do, when
you know all my crimes, or rather
my misfortunes ? Under a fictitious
name I have much abufed your confidence ; I am not whom you think.——
I am—the Count of Comminge.——
What, interrupted Adelaid, are you
our mortal foe ? It is you, it is your
father who purfue with unremitting
hate our family to ruin.——Brand
me not with a name fo odious ; I am
your lover ready to facrifice my fortune and my life in your fervice. My
father fhall not do you evil ; my love
affures you of it.

Why

Why have you thus deceived me,
fays fhe, why dealt thus ungeneroufly
with me ? Had you not deceived me,
I fhould not have been thus unhappy ;
had you difcovered your real name, it
would have taught me to avoid you.

Repent not, replied I, of that goodnefs, you have deigned to fhew me.

Leave me, fays fhe, leave me, the
more I fee, the more I hear, renders
to a greater degree inevitable the
miferies I cannot but apprehend.

The tendernefs of thefe words,
which gave me reafon to hope, filled
my

my foul with joy ineffable. I flattered
myfelf that my father would confent
to my requeft; I was fo full of the
idea, that I thought every one muft
think and feel as I did. I even mentioned my hopes to Adelaid as certain
of fuccefs. I know not, fays fhe, why
my heart refufes thefe amufing hopes;
mifery ftares me in the face; yet I am
happy in feeling, what I feel for you.
I have without referve difclofed my
fentiments; fentiments I am willing
you fhould know; but at the fame
time remember, that I fhall know
when requifite to facrifice them to my
duty.

6

I had

I had previous to my departure frequent converfations with Adelaid, and
had every day new reafons to congratu-
late myfelf on my good fortune. The
pleafure of loving, and the confcioufnefs of being loved, filled all my foul
with joy. Jealoufy difturbed not the
harmony of our difcourfe ; diftruft
interrupted not our future fchemes of
happinefs. We were convinced of
each other's affections, and this cer-
tainty fo far from diminifhing our vi-
vacity, heightened the pleafure of mutual confidence. Adelaid's only inquietude arofe from her apprehenfions
of my father. I fhall die with grief,
fays fhe, if I fhould bring you into
disgrace

difgrace with your family ; I hope
you love me, but I hope you will be
happy. At length the dreadful moment came ; I left her full of the moſt
tender and lively paſſion ; and I buoy-
ed up myſelf with the hopes of ren-
dering my father favourable to my
love.

Alas ! he already was informed of
every circumſtance which had paſſed.
The ſervant he had ſent with me, was
ordered to be a ſpy on my conduct ;
he therefore had acquainted my father
with my love and with my duel: and
had painted the Marchioneſs of Luſſan
and her daughter as artful deſigning
wo-

women, who knew me to be the Count of Comminge, and had enticed me into their fnares. My father, naturally paffionate, was worked up by this information to a paroxyfm of fury ; he treated me on my return with the moft favage inhumanity, and reproached me with my attachment to Adelaid as with a crime of the blackeft enormity.

Bafe wretch, fays he, dare you love my enemies; without any regard to what you owe either yourfelf, or me, you have entered into engagements with a family which my heart abhors. I know not to what lengths your meannefs may have carried you.

D   Yes,

Yes, my father, faid I, I am blame-
able, but I am unavoidably fo. I cannot withftand my fate ; and while I
on my knees implore your pardon,
I feel that no power on earth can detach me from my love. Have pity on
me, I dare repeat, have pity on me !
Finifh this variance, which has im-
bittered the funfhine of your days, and
fuffer yourfelf to be reconciled to the
houfe of Luffan. Our mutual love
the moment we faw each other feems
to be the interpofition of heaven to
effect a reconciliation. You are the
father of none but me ! wifh you to
load me with mifery, aggravated with
the reflection of having received the
cup

oup of bitternefs from the hand of him who gave me life? Have compaffion on a fon who has involuntarily offended!

My father regarded me while I fpake with an eye of indignation; I have heard you, fays he, with a compofure which aftonifhes me, and which I thought myfelf incapable of; the only favour you can expect from me is this alternative; either renounce your folly, or the title of my fon; be fpeedy in your refolves, and inftantly deliver up thofe papers entrufted to your care, a confidence you little merited.

Had

Had my father relented, his demand would have perplexed me much ; but his cruelty gave me courage. The papers, replied I, are no longer in my cuſtody, they are committed to the flames ; let my eſtate indemnify your loſs. Scarce had I ſpoken, when my father, with all the fury of a maniac, drew his ſword, and as I made not the leaſt effort of reſiſtance, he would have inevitably killed me, had not my mother that inſtant entered the apartment, and threw herſelf between us in the moment the father was going to imbrue his hands in the blood of an only child. Know you not your own ſon, cried ſhe ? then turning to

me,

me, ordered me to attend her in her dreffing room.—I waited a confiderable time before my mother appeared; at length fhe came, not armed with rage, nor difguifed by paffion ; fhe looked, fhe fpake the tender parent, who entered into all my pains. She begged me with tears to pity the condition I had reduced her to.

Alas my fon can a miftrefs whom you have fo lately known blot all duty from your memory ?—May not a parent's tears prevail ? If on me your happinefs depended, my life fhould be a willing facrifice. But you my fon have a father who will be obeyed ; he

D 3   is

is now ready to enter into the moſt violent meaſures. If you wiſh not to load me with miſery inſupportable, conquer a paſſion productive of nothing but unhappineſs.——

I knew not what to reply; I loved my mother with all the tenderneſs of filial affection, but my paſſion for Adelaid was too violent to be removed. I ſhould prefer death, ſaid I, to the diſobliging of you ; and die I ſhall, if you have not pity on me. To what would you adviſe me? I can give up life with greater eaſe than Adelaid. Dare I break the vows, the proteſtations I have made? after receiving proofs of

her

her affection, shall I forsake her? No my mother, you cannot wish your son to be a villain.——

I then related the whole progress of my love; I am certain, said I, you would approve of my choice, for she has your sweetness of disposition, she has your openness of heart; can you then wish me to cease loving such amiableness? But, says my mother, what do you purpose to do? Your father insists on your immediately marrying, and you are to be sent into the country till the day arrives. It is therefore absolutely necessary that you appear determined to obey him. You are to

D 4   be

be fent into the country to-morrow, attended by a perfon in whom he can confide.

Abfence may work greater miracles than you imagine ; time may efface the traces of Adelaid's perfeſtions, and you may be again yourſelf. But at all adventures irritate not your fa-ther by diſobedience ; delay the time, if poſſible ; I on my part will leave nothing undone that may give you fatisfaſtion. Your father's diſpoſition has ever been too violent, but now his vengeance is lawful, to what ex-tremes will it not provoke him ? You are highly culpable in deſtroying

thoſe

Women blamed by men — seductress ↑

thofe papers ; and he is perfuaded that Adelaid inveigled you to make her that facrifice by the order of her mother.

Alas faid I, is it poffible he can think fo uncharitably of the Marchionefs of Luffan ! So far from it, that Adelaid knows not what I have done ; and I am confident fhe would have employed all her power over me to have prevented it.

I then concerted a plan of correfpondence, and beged fhe would vifit Adelaid on her arrival at Bourdeaux. She affured me fhe would, on condition

tion that I would implicitly submit to my father, if Adelaid's affection should fall short of my expectations. The greatest part of the night passed away in conversing with my mother, when the morning dawned, my conductor informed me I must mount my horse.

The place of my exile was situated in the mountains, some leagues distant from the Wells; I went therefore part of the same road which I had so lately travelled. As we arrived early the second day of our journey at a village where we were to spend the night, I took a walk on the high-road by way of amusement till supper; I

had

had gone but a small distance, before I observed a carriage, which
through the awkwardness of the driver
was overturned some paces from me.
Not only humanity, but the unusual
fluttering of my heart told me the
part I was to act on the occasion. I
fled to the chariot; two servants who
had quitted their horses assisted me in
relieving the sufferers, whom I found
on enquiry to be Adelaid and her mother. It was them indeed! Adelaid had greatly bruised her foot, but
the pleasure of seeing me made her
forget her pains. She was too lame
to walk; I gently raised her up; I
clasped her in my arms; hers folded
round

round my neck, her hand gently preſſed upon my lips. Not all my miſeries, nor ſo many years of ſorrow can efface from my memory that rapturous moment which gave my Adelaid to my arms. I was in an extacy of joy that near deprived me of ſenſation: Adelaid could not but perceive it; her modeſty took the alarm, and ſhe endeavoured to diſengage herſelf from my embrace. Alas! little ·did ſhe know the exceſs of my love; I was too full of my raptures, to think of aught beſide.

Let me endeavour to walk, ſays ſhe, in a low and timid voice; have

you

5

you then, replied I, the cruelty to
envy me the only happiness perhaps
I shall ever taste? My words were
accompanied with a look of inexpreffible tenderness. She continued filent ;
and one false step intentionally made,
fixed her in her former fituation.

The inn was fo near, that in a few
moments I was deprived of my pre-
cious charge. I carried her to an
apartment, while the fervants took
care of her mother, who was much
more dangeroufly hurt : as they were
bufy in attending on the Marchionefs,
it gave me an opportunity of relating
part

part of the converfation between my father and me.

I fuppreffed the article of having burnt the title deeds, which fhe had not the leaft fufpicion of ;. her knowledge of which would have concerned me much. I dared not paint my father in his proper colours ; for Adelaid was fo ftrictly virtuous, that fhe would have lent a deaf ear to my vows, had fhe not flattered herfelf, that our families would at length confent to our union.

I confirmed her hopes by affuring her of my mother's tendernefs for me,
and

and favourable opinion of her. Adelaid then defired that I would fpeak
to the Marchionefs : " She knows
" your fentiments for me, and is no
" ftranger to the fituation of my heart.
" I thought her authority neceffary to
" affift me in conquering my incli-
" nations, if requifite ; or to let me
" give way to them without control.
" I am confident fhe will leave no ex-
" pedient untried that may effect an
" accommodation."

The joy which thefe hopes gave
Adelaid, made my heart more livelily
fufceptible of its mifery. " Tell me
" replied I, (preffing her hand with
" all

" all the warmth of virtuous love) if
" our fathers fhould prove inexorable,
" will you then have pity on me?
" My utmoft endeavours, fays fhe,
" fhall be exerted to make my incli-
" nations conformable to my duty;
" but I feel, that I fhall be moft
" miferable, if duty fhould oblige
" me to renounce you."

The Marchionefs of Luffan's attendants coming in, interrupted our
converfation. I immediately paid my
refpects to the old lady, who received
me with great cordiality, and promifed to leave nothing undone, which

could

could contribute to the reconcilement of our families.

On this affurance I withdrew, and fearched after my conductor who waited for me in my chamber. As he had not had the curiofity to enquire the ftrangers names, I had an opportunity of feeing Adelaid once again before my departure. I the next morning entered her chamber in a fituation which beggars all defcription; the idea of taking leave perhaps for ever chilled my blood with horror. I approached her mother, my voice faultered, I could not fpeak! but grief was a powerful advocate, and fo fuc-

E   cefsfully

cefsfully plead ed my caufe, that I was honoured with more particular marks of efteem than the preceding evening. Adelaid was retired to the other end of the room ; it was with difficulty I could fupport myfelf ; I at length drew near and attempted to fpeak, but could only fay, my deareft Adelaid, muft I leave you ? my tears fpoke the reft —I have, fays fhe, (the fympathizing tear ftealing down her cheek) already fhewed you the fenfibility of my heart ; I repent not of it. The purity of my thoughts authorizes my freedom, and you merit my utmoft good opinion.. What will be our fate I know not. My parents muft decide mine.—

mine.——Why, replied I, fhould we fubmit to the tyranny of our parents? Let us treat them as they deferve? Let us fly to the extremeft corner of the earth, and enjoy in retirement the fweets of mutual love.

How dare you, anfwered Adelaid, affront me with fuch a propofal? Would you have me repent of my choice, would you that I fhould recal my favourable opinion of you? I have already confeffed that my tendernefs may render me miferable, but depend on it it fhall never make me criminal. Adieu, added fhe, (offering me her hand) and remember that by

E 2 our

our conftancy and our virtue we muft
engage the fmiles of fortune; but
however we may be difpofed of, let
us refolve to do nothing which may
make us blufh for each other.

I kiffed her hand as fhe fpake; I
bathed it with my tears: I attempted
to fpeak, but my tongue refufed its
office. My heart was fo full, that I
quitted her apartment without making any reply.

I inftantly mounted my horfe, and
rode the whole day without fuftenance,
and without ceafing to weep. At
length my tears abated, and I began

to

to taſte the tranquillity which reſults from a conſciouſneſs of being tenderly beloved.———

The remainder of our journey paſſed as the beginning, in an uninterrupted ſilence.———We arrived on the third day at a caſtle built at the bottom of the Pyrenees, which was deſtined for my retreat.—Groves of cypreſs and barren rocks were all my view, and I heard nothing but the croaking of the ravens and the thunder of the cataracts which fell from the mountains.———

E 3

This situation, all savage as it was, gave me much satisfaction. For the gloominess of the prospect fed the melancholy of my mind. I spent whole days in the woods, writing the effusions of my love; this was my only pleasure, this was my sole employ.

I heard sometimes from my mother, and in one letter she gave me a gleam of hope, by telling me that all our relations were labouring at an accommodation, and that she had reason to think their endeavours would not be ineffectual. For the ensuing six weeks I had no letter from my mother; good God!

God! how tedious were those days to me. I walked conftantly upon the road the meffenger muft come, and returned as conftantly difappointed. At length I faw at fome diftance a man whofe bufinefs I doubted not was with me. My former impatience vanifhed, and gave way to fear. I dared not advance to meet him, my feet were riveted to the ground. The doubts the anxiety which appeared before fo infupportable, feemed at that inftant to be a bleffing I was foon to be deprived of.

I was not deceived.——The letters brought me by this meffenger, inform-

ed

ed me that my father would not liſten
to any terms ; and to add to the ful-
neſs of my miſery, I moreover learned
that he finally had fixed my marriage
with a daughter of the Count of Foix ;
that the nuptials were to be celebrated
at the place of my confinement, and that
he would be with me in a few days to
prepare for the ſolemnity.   I did not
heſitate one moment on the part I was
to act ; I expected my father's arrival
with compoſure ; and it was ſome
mitigation to my pains to be enabled
to make Adelaid this ſacrifice.   I was
well aſſured of her fidelity ; I loved
too much to doubt it.   Love like
mine was a ſtranger to ſuſpicion.—

4   My

My mother likewise who had such cogent reasons to detach me from Adelaid, had never even hinted in her letters the least suspicion of her inconstancy.—

Adelaid's fidelity contributed to the liveliness of my passion, and I was more enabled to meet my father's severity, as it gave me an opportunity of shewing my affection. The three days previous to my father's arrival, I passed in settling my plan of behaviour, which would give Adelaid fresh instances of my constancy. This idea in spite of my deplorable situation, filled

filled my heart with a senfation bordering on joy.——

The interview between my father
and me was on my part very cool,
but refpectful; on his, ftern and
haughty.

I have given you time, fays he, to
repent of your follies, and now am
come to give you an opportunity to
atone for them. Let your obedience
be your reply to this mark of my
goodnefs, and prepare to receive as
your wife the lady I have deftined for
you. The marriage fhall be here;
your mother will arrive to-morrow
with

with the Count of Foix and his daughter. I am extremely forry, Sir, (faid I) that it is not in my power to oblige you. I have too much honour to give my hand, where my heart will ever be a ftranger. I beg your permiffion therefore to leave this place; fince Mademoifelle de Foix, all amiable as fhe may be, will not be able to fhake my refolution : and the ill compliment I muft pay her, will be felt more fenfibly in refufing her hand, after I fhall be acquainted with her perfon ; let me intreat you therefore to detain me no longer in this place.

No,

No, replies my father, with fury flashing from his eye, you shall not go, neither shall you more behold the sun; for I will instantly confine you in a dungeon, destined for the reception of such as you.—I swear no power on earth shall ever set you at liberty, unless you return to your duty. I will punish you by every method my vengeance can suggest; I will disinherit you, I will strip you of your fortune, and give it to Mademoiselle de Foix, that I may keep my word with her as much as in my power. His threat was instantly executed, and I was conducted to

the

the bottom of a tower, which admitted only a glimmering light through a small iron grate in the wall. He ordered me to be moſt narrowly watched, to be fed but twice in the day, and to be ſecluded from all intercourſe with my friends or relations.

In this ſtate did I paſs ſome days not wholly devoid of ſatisfaction. The ſacrifice I had made Adelaid ſo entirely engroſſed my attention, that I paid no regard to the inconveniences of a priſon. But when this reflection became leſs lively on my imagination, I gave way to all the agonies of grief; I tortured myſelf with apprehenſions that

that Adelaid might be forced into new engagements. I painted her as surrounded with my rivals assiduous in their devoirs, while I was immured in a dungeon, the companion of affliction. Recollection checked such rebel thoughts, and my heart smote me for harbouring suspicions of that ungenerous nature.

My mother contrived to convey a letter to me, in which she exhorted me to obey my father, whose resentment grew every day more violent. She added, that she had suffered greatly on my account, and that her assiduity in attempting a reconciliation

had

had made my father fufpect her correfpondence.

My mother's uneafinefs gave me
frefh concern, but I thought my own
fufferings would in fome meafure excufe my behaviour. As I was thus
meditating on the feverity of my fate,
I was interrupted in my revery, by a
noife at the window, and immediately
a letter dropped into the room. I
broke it open with anxiety bordering
on diftraction, I was motionlefs with
apprehenfion ; but what became of
me after I had read it ? Thefe were
the contents.————

"I am

" I am indebted to the Count of
" Comminge for the knowledge of
" my obligations to you, which his
" anger provoked him to difcover,
" and which your generofity would
" never have revealed. I am like-
" wife but too well acquainted with
" the horrors of your fituation, from
" which you cannot be relieved, but
" by means which probably may
" heighten your mifery. Your ge-
" nerofity requires the moft grateful
" return ; gratitude enables me to ex-
" ecute, what your fufferings moft
" juftly demand. Your father infifts,
" that the price of your liberty fhall
" be my immediate marriage, as that
                                    " will

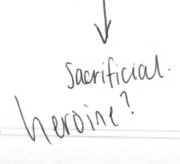

Sacrificial.
heroine?

" will effectually prevent the union
" fo odious to his thoughts. The fa-
" crifice may perhaps coft me my
" life, moft certainly my peace of
" mind for ever. Not mifery in all
" its variety of horrors fhall aught
" avail, I am determined! Your fuf-
" ferings, your imprifonment, are
" ever before my eyes. In a few
" days I fhall be the wife of the Mar-
" quis of Benavides. That which I
" know of his character, tells me
" what I am to undergo. But at
" leaft I owe you this mark of my
" fidelity, that I can from my en-
" gagement forefee nothing but mi-
" fery. You, on the contrary, en-

F   " deavour

" deavour to be happy. Your eafe
" and tranquillity will be my only
" confolation. I ought not to have
" faid fo much. Was I truely ge-
" nerous, my motive for marrying
" fhould be to you unknown, that
" you might call ingratitude, what
" arifes from excefs of love. I had
" formed fuch a defign, but wanted
" courage to put it in execution. In
" my deplorable fituation, I need the
" confolation of thinking, that my
" memory will not be odious to you.
" Alas ! how foon muft I banifh all
" thoughts of you. I muft forget
" you ; I muft at leaft attempt it.
" But my mifery, however keen, will
" be

" be more fenfibly aggravated, if you
" do not moft ftudioufly avoid all
" occafion of feeing or fpeaking to
" me. Remember, that you owe me
" this mark of your efteem; and
" think how dear that efteem muft
" be to me, fince that is the only
" fentiment virtue will permit me to
" demand."——

Of this fatal epiftle, I read only
to thefe words, " Your father infifts,
" that the price of your liberty fhall
" be my immediate marriage." That
dreadful fentence penetrated me with
fuch a lively grief, that I could read
no more. I threw myfelf on a mat-

F 2   trefs,

trefs, which was the whole furniture of my bed, where I laid for some hours without fenfation, and probably had clofed my eyes for ever, had it not been for the affiftance of the fervant who brought my food. He was greatly alarmed at the ftate he found me in, but much more fo at the excefs of my forrow, when I recovered my fenfes. The letter, which during my fwoon, I had held faft in my hand, was bathed with my tears, and I fpoke fo incoherently, that he was under apprehenfions for my reafon.—

This man, who before was dead to every fentiment of compaffion, could

not

not now refift the feelings of humanity.
He condemned the proceedings of my
father, he reproached himfelf for ex-
ecuting his orders, and with much
fincerity implored my pardon. His
penitence prompted me to afk his
connivance at my abfence for eight
days only; at the expiration of which
term, I gave him my honour, I would
return and deliver myfelf into his
hands. My gaoler grown compaffionate by my fufferings, ftimulated by
his intereft, and probably apprehenfive of my future vengeance, was
bribed to confent, on condition he
might attend me.

My

My defign, as foon as formed, I wifhed to execute, but no horfes were in readinefs, I therefore reluctantly waited for the enfuing morning. My intention was to fee Adelaid, to difplay all the horrors of my defpair, and on her perfifting in her refolution, to die at her feet.——It was neceffary for the execution of my purpofe to arrive before her marriage; every moment therefore of delay appeared an age. I red over the letter again and again; hoping to find fomething, which might before have efeaped my notice. I examined the date; and flattered myfelf, that this fatal marriage might be delayed.

" She

" She has made this effort, said I, to
" fhew her generofity ; but undoubt-
" edly fhe will feize every pretext to
" defer it.   But how can I flatter my-
" felf with fuch idle chimeras ? Ade-
" laid facrififes herfelf to my liberty,
" fhe therefore will expedite the
" day.——Alas ! how could fhe fup-
" pofe that liberty alone had any
" charms for me ? No—I fhall every
" where find that prifon from which fhe
" wifhes to deliver me.————She never
" knew my love.————She views me
" through the falfe medium of other
" men.——Yes————there is the rock on
" which I fplit————I am yet more
" miferable than my gloomy imagi-

F 4   " nation

" nation painted me ; for now I have
" loft the confolation of thinking,
" that fhe was confcious of the excefs
" of my paffion." The whole night
was paffed in plaints like thefe. As
foon as the morning dawned, I mounted my fteed, and rode the whole day
a ftranger to refrefhment. I was towards the evening unexpectedly met
by my mother, who having teftified
her furprife at the unexpected meeting,
infifted on my getting into her carriage. I dared not enquire the occafion of her journey; I feared the worft ;
my fears were too well founded.———

I come

I come, says she, my son, with your
father's consent, to deliver you from
your imprisonment. Alas, said I,
Adelaid is married! My mother answered only by her silence.——My
misfortunes which were now irremedi-
able burst upon me in all their horrors.
I fell into a state of insensibility, and
such was the power of grief, that my
mind was alike indifferent to every
sensation. Neither was my body a
stranger to pain. I was seized with a
shivering fit while we were in the chariot: my mother, as soon as we alighted,
ordered me to bed. The two following days I laid without speaking, without nourishment.——My fever in-
creased,

creafed, and the third day I was
thought beyond the power of phyfic.
My mother never left my chamber;
her tears, her intreaties, and the name
of Adelaid, by which fhe often invoked
me, at length prevailed on me to live.
After five days the fury of the fever
abated. My firft enquiry was for
Adelaid's letter, which my mother
had taken away during my phrenzy.
She perceived I was fo affected with
the lofs of it, that fhe was obliged to
return it. I put it into a purfe which
contained Adelaid's picture, and feized
every opportunity to retire and read
it.———

My

My mother, who was by nature compaſſionate, ſympathized with me, and endeavoured to ſooth my cares; ſhe knew the neceſſity of humouring my grief, and that the cure muſt be left to time. She ſuffered me to talk of Adelaid, and often herſelf would begin the converſation. And as ſhe found that the only thing which adminiſtered conſolation, was the idea of my beloved, ſhe minutely related to me her perſuading Adelaid to marry.——

" I implore your pardon, my ſon,
" for the misfortune I have unhappily
" brought on you; and which I

4

" could not apprehend would have so
" senſibly affected you. Your impri-
" ſonment made me fear not only for
" your health, but your life. I was
" no ſtranger to the inflexibility of
" your father, who would never have
" ſet you at liberty, while there was
" a poſſibility of your marrying Ade-
" laid. I was determined to ſpeak to
" that generous girl. I wiſhed her to
" partake of my fears ; ſhe looked
" not on them as the trifling appre-
" henſions of maternal fondneſs, but
" ſeemed more ſenſibly affected than
" myſelf. She deemed my reaſons
" ſo powerful, that ſhe reſolved im-
" mediately to marry. To which her

" duty

" duty contributed not a little ; for
" her father refenting the ufage of
" the Count of Comminge, preffed
" her to give her hand to the worthieft
" of your rivals. I afked her whom
" fhe intended to honour by her
" choice. It is to me, faid fhe, to-
" tally indifferent, fince I cannot give
" my hand to him who has long pof-
" feffed my heart."——

Two days after this converfation, I
heard that the Marquis of Benavides
was preferred to all his rivals. This
was to all a matter of aftonifhment ;
for Benavides perfon is odious to a
degree, which his meannefs of fpirit
and

and capricious humour have rendered
still more despicable. I dread the consequences !—I saw and spake to her a
few days previous to her nuptials.
" I am, said she, preparing myself
" for misery ; but marry I must and
" will.   And since I am confident
" that there is no other step to deliver
" your son, I reproach myself for
" every moment's delay. Yet this
" marriage, which is solely for his
" welfare, will probably be the most
" intolerable of my miseries. I shall
" at least convince him by my choice,
" that his interest alone determined
" me.   Pity me, my dear madam, for
" I deserve your compassion ; by my
                    " behaviour

" behaviour to the Marquis of Be-
" navides I will merit your esteem."
My mother added, that the Count of
Comminge had acquainted Adelaid
with my burning the title deeds, and
publickly reproached her for it. She
solemnly declared to me, says my mother, that nothing so sensibly touched
her as your generosity in concealing
the favour you had conferred on her
family. *takes blame.*

Our time passed away in such like
converse, and although my melancholy
was excessive, it yet had that inex-
pressible sweetness, which attends the
consciousness of being beloved. Some
months

months had elapsed, when my mother received a letter from my father, ordering her immediate return. He had scarce deigned to take any notice of my illness; for such had been his behaviour to me, that it had entirely estranged his affections. My mother pressed me to return, but I begged leave to continue in the country, to which, after much importunity, she assented.

I was determined to live the life of a recluse, and should never have quitted my solitude, had it not been for the tender affection I owed my mother. Sometimes I formed schemes to see

Adelaid,

2

Adelaid, which the fear of difobliging her as often prevented. After wavering thus for fome days, I reafoned myfelf into a belief of the innocence of feeing her, if without her knowledge or confent.——

I was fo riveted to this fcheme, that I determined to fend my fervant to Bourdeaux to enquire after the Marquis of Benavides family. This man had lived with me from my infancy, had waited on me at the Wells, and during my illnefs had been again permitted to attend me. After having given him all requifite inftructions, and repeated them to him again and

G   again,

again, I suffered him to depart. On his arrival at Bourdeaux, he learned that the Marquis was not there, but had retired into the country with his lady soon after their marriage.—My servant, who had assumed the name of St. Laurent, wrote to me for further orders. I ordered him to Biscay, the country seat of Benavides without loss of time, for my impatience to see Adelaid was grown irresistible. St. Laurent was near six weeks on his journey. On his return he told me, that after much trouble and variety of fruitless schemes, he at length gained admittance into the house in the character of an architect, that he fortunately

nately

nately underftood the bufinefs, having been originally educated to it, and that the Marquis of Benavides was in great want of fuch a perfon.——" I believe, " added he, that madam de Benavides " recollected me; certain am I at leaft, " that my firft appearance called up a " blufh on her countenance." He informed me, that fhe lived the moft retired and melancholy life ; that her hufband was perpetually with her, was fond of her to excefs, but that jealoufy was the only proof he had given her of his affections ; which he carried to fuch lengths, that his own brother was not permitted to fee her, fave only in his prefence.————

I found

I found, on enquiry, that this brother was a young gentleman the very
reverfe of the Marquis, and was as
univerfally efteemed as the other was
defpifed; and that he appeared much
attached to his fifter-in law. This information did not immediately make
any impreffion on me. The deplorable fituation of madam de Benavides,
and my anxiety to fee her, engroffed
my whole attention. St. Laurent faid,
he had taken proper meafures for my
introduction; that I muft affume the
character of a painter, as the Marquis had ordered him to bring an
adept in that art. Nothing more
was requifite than to prepare for our
journey.——

journey.—I wrote to my mother,
and informed her, that I was going
to spend a few weeks at a friend's
house. I then immediately with St.
Laurent took the road to Bifcay.
There was no end to my enquiries
about madam de Benavides, 1 wifhed
to hear the minuteft trifles which concerned her. St. Laurent could give
me but little fatisfaction, as he had fel-
dom feen her. He faid, fhe paffed
whole days in her own apartment, with
no other company but a little dog,
which fhe feemed extravagantly fond
of. This circumftance gave me pe-
culiar pleafure, as I had prefented the
dog to her ; and I flattered myfelf,

that

enjoys her sadness.

that she caressed him on that account.
When a man is truely wretched, he
dwells on every trifle which fleeted
by unnoticed in the sunshine of prosperity. The heart, which needeth consolation, catches at every shadow.
St. Laurent spake much of young Benavides attachment to his sister, that
he often soothed his brother's passions, and that he contributed greatly
to the relief of Adelaid's melancholy.
He exhorted me not to attempt speaking to her. I do not, said he, mention the danger of a discovery, since
your own danger would be too trifling
a motive to restrain you; but consider that you will expose her, who is
dearer

2

dearer to you than life, to the fury of a jealous and implacable hufband. I was perfuaded, that the feeing of Adelaid would be fo great a fatisfaction, that I fhould not wifh to fpeak to her; I therefore gave my word to St. Laurent, that my circumfpection fhould outftrip his fears.

After many days journey, which appeared years to my impatience, we arrived in fafety at Bifcay, where I was introduced to the Marquis, and immediately employed. I was lodged with the pretended architect, whofe bufinefs was to fuperintend the works. I continued my employ for many days

G 4   without

sneaky

without feeing the object of my foul.
At length I faw the dear lovely Adelaid pafs the window of the room in
which I was painting. The evening
was fine, and fhe was walking in the
garden with the little dog, but feemed
indifferent to the pleafing objects
round. There was in her gait an air
of languor, and melancholy was feated
on her brow. My God! how can I
defcribe the anguifh of my foul? I
remained like a ftatue at the window
waiting her return; when it was fo
late, that I could not diftinguifh her
as fhe paffed; but my heart told me
it was Adelaid.——

The

The second time I saw her was in the chapel. I had so placed myself, that I could remark every action unobserved. I never once could catch her eye, for which I ought to have been thankful ; as she most assuredly would have obliged me to leave the house. Yet I was affected at having escaped her notice, and returned from the chapel more sick at heart, more heavily oppressed, than when I entered it. I had as yet contrived no plan for discovering myself, but was afraid, that if occasion offered, my integrity would yield to the temptation.

Young

Young Benavides likewife gave me much uneafinefs. He was often with me, and notwithftanding the apparent difference of our fituations, treated me with a familiarity which required at leaft my gratitude. But his agreeable behaviour and extraordinary merit, which I could not but obferve, reftrained my acknowledgments. I dreaded in him a rival, and perceived in the whole tenor of his behaviour, a fpecies of melancholy too nearly refembling mine, not to fufpect the caufe from which it fprang. But what wedded me to my fufpicions, was his faying that I was in love. The melancholy, faid he, with which I fee

you

you oppreffed arifes from the heart. Can I ferve you? Speak your wants, it will be to me a fatisfaction to relieve them. The unfortunate in general meet with my compaffion, but yours is a misfortune which I more particularly pity.——

I thanked the Chevalier for his obliging offers with an ill grace. I could not deny my love ; but told him, that fuch was my fituation, that time alone muft work the cure. If faid he you can expect that, I am no ftranger to a perfon yet more miferable than yourfelf.

When

. When he was retired, I made a thousand reflections on our preceding conversation. I concluded that he was in love, and that his sister was the object of his affections. Every circumstance, which I most minutely examined, confirmed me in my suspicions. I saw that he was attached to Adelaid, and that he looked at her with my eyes. Yet I was not jealous. My esteem for Adelaid banished such ungenerous sentiments from my heart: but I could not suppress my fears, that the sight of an amiable young man, ever studious to oblige, might diminish her regard for

me,

Men seek her
without her efforts

me, who was the innocent but unhappy author of all her woes.

My thoughts were in this train,
when Adelaid attended by the Chevalier, entered the apartment I was
painting. I cannot conceive, said she,
why you prefs me thus to fee the al-
terations which are making in this
room ? You know I have no tafte for
painting.——I truft madam, said I,
looking full upon her, that if you will
condefcend to obferve this painting,
you will not repent your complaifance.
Adelaid ftruck with my voice immediately knew me.——She trembled,
turned pale, and obferving that the
smell

smell of the paint was disagreeable, left the apartment without deigning me the least regard.

I was motionless with astonishment, and overwhelmed with grief. "What "have I done? It is true indeed I "have disobeyed her orders; but if "she loved me, she would pardon "a crime which tends only to shew "the excess of my passion."

I hastily therefore concluded, that since Adelaid did not love me, she must necessarily love another. This thought drove me even to madness. From that moment only did I date

my

compare to Scudéry akmant
Malhereux

my misery. St. Laurent entered the
room and found me in an agitation,
which filled him with apprehension.
" What is the matter, said he, what
" accident has happened ?"

" I am undone, Adelaid loves me
" not. I again repeated, Adelaid
" loves me not. Is it possible ? Alas !
" from this cruel moment have I not
" reason to complain. What misery,
" what torture would I not undergo
" to recal the happiness I have lost ?
" That happiness, which was all in
" all to me ; that happiness, which
" made me smile in misery."—

St. Laurent

St. Laurent could not comprehend
from my broken fentences and wild
tranfports of complaint, what was
the occafion of them. I was at length
fufficiently compofed to give him information. I do not, faid he, apprehend, that you have juft caufe to
drive you to defpair. Madam de Benavides is undoubtedly offended at
the ftep you have taken, and intends
by her indifference to punifh you for
it. Befides fhe might be afraid of
difcovering you, had fhe feemed to
regard you.—No, no, replied I, love
has not that command over itfelf.
Love is not thus circumfpectly pru-
dent. The heart obeys its firft impulfe.

pulſe. I muſt ſee her, I muſt reproach her with her inconſtancy.
Alas! after what ſhe has done, ought
ſhe in this cruel manner to rob
me of my life? Why did ſhe not
ſuffer me to remain in priſon? then I
had been happy; for then I ſhould
have thought myſelf beloved.

St. Laurent, afraid that any one
ſhould ſee me in that deplorable condition, conducted me to my chamber.
I ſpent the whole night in torments
inexpreſſible. I had no ſooner formed
an idea, than it gave way to ſome new
phantom of my brain. One moment
I condemned my ſuſpicions as un-

H   generous,

generous, and nourished them as re-
alities the next. Now I acknowledged my injustice in wishing Adelaid
to preserve a tenderness, which
must be productive of misery;
then I reproached my selfishness
in loving her less for her sake
than my own. " Since she loves me
" no more, said I to St. Laurent,
" since she has transferred her af-
" fection, I will breath out my soul
" at her feet; but before death shall
" close my eye, will bid her a last
" adieu; one tender, last farewel:
" she shall hear no reproach from me.
" My grief, which cannot be sup-
                              " pressed,

death manipulative !!!

" preffed, will more than fufficiently
" reproach her."

I fortified myfelf in this refolution,
and was determined to put it into execution. St. Laurent told me to take
the opportunity, while the Chevalier
was hunting, and when the Marquis
was engaged with his fteward: and
made me promife, the better to lull
fufpicion afleep, to work as ufual,
and to talk of my approaching departure.

I refumed my brufh, and flattered
myfelf that Adelaid would pay me
another vifit. Every footftep awoke

my

my attention; every noife alarmed me. I had been in this ftate of anxious expectation for fome days, and had almoft bidden adieu to hope; I therefore was determined to feize the firft moment of her being alone. That moment at length arrived. I faw Adelaid enter her chamber alone; I knew that the Chevalier was engaged in hunting, and that the Marquis was in an under room with one of his tenants. I followed Adelaid with fuch precipitation, that fhe did not immediately obferve me; fhe would have fled the moment fhe faw me, had I not detained her by catching hold of her robe; " Fly me not madam, faid I,
" let

forceful3

" let me for a moment enjoy your
" presence?—— That instant past,
" and I will trouble you no more.—
" I will leave you, for ever leave you;
" and expiate by my death the mi-
" series I have occasioned you. For
" I cannot, will not survive the loss
" of your affections. I hope the
" Chevalier will be more fortunate
" than - - - - - - - Adelaid, whom
" surprise and anxiety had hitherto
" kept silent, interrupted me at these
" words, and casting a scornful look
" at me, dare you, says she, re-
" proach me? Dare you suspect me?
" You - - - - - No, my lovely Ade-
" laid, replied I, throwing myself

H 3

" at

strong.

" at her feet, I harbour no injurious
" fufpicions; pardon the words, to
" which my heart affented not."

I pardon you from my very foul,
faid fhe, but leave me immediately,
and never fee me more; confider, that
it is for you, and you alone, that I am
the moft miferable of all human be-
ings, wifh you to make me the moft
criminal?——Your orders, replied I,
fhall be moft religioufly obferved;
but promife me at leaft, that you hate
me not.——

I ftill continued kneeling, although
Adelaid had entreated me to rife.

2   Thofe

[111]

Thofe who love, can be no ftrangers
to the charms of that engaging attitude.   I was yet in that pofture, when
the door opened, and the Marquis,
with his fword drawn, rufhed in upon
us.————You die, wretch, fays he to
his wife, you fhall this moment die.
His threat would have been immediately executed, had I not thrown myfelf between them, drawing my fword
at the fame inftant.   " I will begin
" my vengeance then with you, ac-
" companying his words with a thruft,
" which wounded me in the fhoulder.
" Life for its own fake was not
" worth defending; but I hated Be-
" nevides too much to yield it up

H 4   " a fa-

" a facrifice to his fury. Befides, his in-
" tent to murder his wife had made
" me deaf to the voice of reafon;
" I returned the affault, and in a mo-
" ment left him motionlefs on the
" floor."

The domefticks, alarmed by the
cries of Madam de Benavides, entered
the room the inftant I was withdraw-
ing my fword from their mafter's body.
They fell on me, and difarmed me
without the leaft refiftance. The fight
of Madam de Benavides proftrate on
the floor, and weeping over her bleeding hufband deprived me of every
                                sentiment

fentiment but grief. I was draged
from the chamber, and fecured.

Then I faw (when left to my reflections) the abyfs into which I had
plunged my Adelaid. Her hufband
killed before her eyes, and killed by
me, could not fail encouraging fufpicions injurious to her reputation.
What had I not to reproach myfelf
with ? To me fhe owed the birth of
her misfortunes, which my impru-
dence had now completed. → ruins her life

" She ought to hate me ; I juftly
" merit it. My fole remaining hope
" was, that I fhould not be known.
                              " The

" The idea of being thought a villain,
" which on any other occasion would
" have chilled my soul with horror,
" had now no fears for me. Adelaid,
" said I, will do me justice, and Ade-
" laid is all the world to me."

This thought administered me some
tranquillity; which, my impatience
to answer their interrogatories interrupted. At midnight my door opened, and the Chevalier surprised me
by his presence. Fear not, says he,
I wait on you by Madam de Benavides order. Such is her opinion of
me, that she has concealed nothing
respecting you.—Probably, added he

with

with a figh, which would not be fuppreffed, had fhe known me better,
fhe would not have been thus explicit;
notwithftanding that, I will not be-
tray her confidence; if poffible, I will
fave you both.——You fhall not, faid
I, fave me, had I thoufand lives, I
would facrifice them to Madam de
Benanides juftification.

I then explained my defign of remaining unknown, and fuffering as
an affaffin. Your fcheme, repl.ed the
Chevalier, might be feafible, were my
brother dead, which from your converfation, I perceive, you apprehend.
But his wound, though dangerous, is

not

not mortal. And the firſt ſign he
gave of life, was his order to confine
his wife in her own apartment. That
may be ſufficient to convince you of his
ſuſpicions, you will therefore throw
away your life an uſeleſs ſacrifice. Fly
therefore immediately ; I can do to
night what will not be in my power
to-morrow.————

What, ſaid I, then will be the fate of
Madam de Benavides ? I cannot prevail
on myſelf to withdraw from the danger which I have brought on her,
and leave her to the mercy of her un-
relenting huſband. I have already,
replied the Chevalier, told you that
your

put her in danger
out of selfishness

your prefence can only render her
fituation ftill more dreadful. Since
Madam de Benavides infifts on it, and
her intereft requires it, I will abfcond!
But I hoped by the facrifice of my
life, to gain her pity, though her
pity I do not merit.—I am a wretch
unworthy even to die for her. Pro-
tect her Chevalier, you are generous,
you are humane; her innocence, her
misfortunes, plead powerfully for her.
You may judge, anfwered he, by
what has inadvertently, or rather unavoidably efcaped me, that Madam
de Benavides intereft is fo dear to my
repofe, that I fhall dedicate my life
to her fervice. Alas! I fhould think
my

.my fervices amply recompenfed, if I could flatter myfelf that fhe had never loved. But who, that has not fuffered like you, can hope to touch a heart like hers.——But go, continued he, profit by the darknefs. He took me by the hand, and led me through the courts of the caftle.

I was fo full of indignation at my own behaviour, that in a phrenzy of defpair, I prayed, if it was poffible to be yet more miferable.

The Chevalier at my departure advifed me to go into a convent of religious at fome fmall diftance. There, faid

said he, you must remain for some days to elude the search I shall be necessitated to make. I have in this letter recommended you to the head of the order, in him you may most implicitly confide.

I loitered for some time about the invirons of the castle unable to prevail on myself to remove. But the hopes of hearing news of Adelaid determined me to proceed to the convent.

I arrived there at day break, and delivered my recommendation to the Abbot, who conducted me to a chamber.

ber. My extreme weakneſs, and my clothes ſtained with blood, made him ſuſpect that I was wounded. Before he could aſk me the queſtion I had ſwooned away. The ſurgeon of the convent was immediately ſent for to examine my wound, which was much inflamed by the ſharpneſs of the night, and irritated by the fatigue I had undergone. When I was alone with the father, to whom I had been recommended, I begged him to ſend to the village for St. Laurent, who, I did apprehend was concealed there. My ſuſpicion was well founded.—St. Laurent returned with the meſſenger. The poor fellow's affliction on hearing

that

that I was wounded, was exceffive.
When he approached my bed, I told
him if he would fave my life, he
muft enquire into Madam de Benavides fituation, and acquaint himfelf
with every particular; for that my
fufferings were more dreadful than
death itfelf in all its horrors. He
promifed to execute my commands
with fidelity and difpatch, and left
me to prepare his meafures. A
fever attacked me with great violence,
my wound grew dangerous, and I
twice fubmitted my fhoulder to the
incifions of the furgeon. But fuch
was the diforder of my mind, that
I regarded not the malady of my body.

I   Madam

Madam de Benavides was ever before my eyes, weeping and proſtrated on the floor by her wounded huſband, in the ſame diſmal attitude as when I left her chamber. I reviewed the miſfortunes of her life; I found myſelf the author of them all: Her marriage, her choice of a huſband in every reſpect odious, theſe were ſacrifices made for me; for me who had filled up the meaſure of her misfortunes by ruining her reputation. I reflected on my ill founded jealouſy, which though it vaniſhed at a word and died in its very birth, I could not pardon.—What a baſe ungenerous ſuſpicion! Adelaid ought to look on me,

as

as on a wretch unworthy her esteem. I must be odious to her memory! This idea all dreadful as it was, the rage with which I was animated against myself enabled me to support. In eight days St. Laurent returned with news ill adapted to calm the transports of my grief. He told me that the Marquis continued in a very dangerous situation; that his wife appeared inconsolable, and that his brother affected searching after me with vigour. As every incident was unpropitious, death should have been my only wish; but I thought I ought to live for Madam de Benavides justification.

The

The Abbot, a witnefs to my fighs and tears, took pity on me. He was a man of addrefs, well acquainted with the world, and had much philanthropy in his difpofition. But a variety of accidents had at length fixed him in a cloifter. He fuccefsfully endeavoured to gain my friendfhip by his fenfibility, and by degrees he won my confidence. He became fo neceffary to my eafe, that I could not confent to his leaving me for a moment. I related to him my misfortunes—I never faw a man with more goodnefs of heart.—I repeated the fame ftory a thoufand times; as often he feemed to hear me with attention,

attention, to enter into all my sorrows, and partake of all my cares. I was indebted to him for the knowledge of what passed at the Marquis's house. He told me that Benavides was declared to be out of danger, that Madam de Benavides lived more than usually retired, and was thought to be in a declining way. He added, that it was necessary I should prepare for my departure as soon as possible least my retreat should be discovered, which would bring fresh troubles on Madam de Benavides.

I was as yet unable to travel, for my fever had never left me, and my

I 3   wound

wound was ftill unhealed. I had been in the convent upwards of two months, when I obferved Don Jerome to be more than ufually thoughtful.——His brow was clouded with care ; he feared to catch my eye, and ftudioufly avoided all converfe with me. The unhappy are ever moft compaffionate ! but for him I had a moft fincere efteem, therefore was going to enquire the caufe of his uneafinefs, when St. Laurent entered my chamber, and told me that the Chevalier was in the convent and had enquired for me.——

He here ! and you not mention him Don Jerome ? I tremble for Madam

dam de Benavides.——For pity's fake
eafe me of the cruel anxiety with
which I am tortured even to madnefs.
After fome hefitation faid Don Jerome embracing me, I wifh with all
my foul that I could for ever eafe
you of your pain.——

"Alas, cried I, Adelaid is dead!
"Benavides has facrificed her to his
"revenge.——You anfwer not—I
"have then no hope.——No—it is not
"Benavides, it is I who plunged
"the poniard into her heart.——Had
"it not been for me, fhe yet had lived.
"My Adelaid is dead! has clofed
"her eyes for ever! No more fhall I
I 4   "behold

" behold her ! She is gone, for ever
" gone ! She is dead ! and yet I live !
" Why do I not follow her ? Why
" do I not revenge her death ? But
" no ! to die will be a joy ; since the
" grave will fwallow up all my cares.
" I will live, and be my own avenger.

" My violent agitation burft open
" my wound, which was not per-
" fectly clofed; it bled again, and
" I fell into fo deep a fwoon, that
" they thought me dead, but after
" fome hours I revived. Don Je-
" rome was apprehenfive I fhould
" attempt my life, and charged St.
" Laurent not to leave me for a mo-
" ment.

" ment. My defpair took another
" turn.—I obferved a mournful fi-
" lence, but never fhed a tear. Then
" it was that I determined to bid a-
" dieu to fociety, and deliver myfelf
" a prey to melancholy. The idea
" of tormenting myfelf was not wholly
" devoid of pleafure. I therefore
" begged to fee the Chevalier
" D'orfanne, as his prefence would
" renew my pain."

He came and feated himfelf by
my bed. For fome time we remained
filent. He looked at me with eyes
furcharged with tears. At length I
fpake.—You are too generous, Sir,

in

in pitying a wretch you ought to hate. But I beg you will not conceal one circumſtance of woe. I ſhall, anſwered he, only add to your miſery and my own ; but as you inſiſt on it, will gratify your curioſity ; when you will know, that you are not alone un-happy, ſince in my recital I ſhall be obliged to make mention of myſelf.—

" I had never ſeen Madam de Be-
" navides before her marriage ; my
" brother, who was engaged in buſi-
" neſs of conſequence at Bourdeaux,
" became her lover; and although
" he had many rivals in every re-
" ſpect preferable to himſelf, yet by

I know

" I know not what fatality, on him
" she fixed her choice. Soon after
" the nuptials, they came into the
" country; it was there I first saw her.
" I admired her person, but was en-
" amoured with the graces of her
" mind. Yet the regard I had for
" an amiable woman whom I ten-
" derly loved, steeled me against her
" charms. My brother would not
" consent to our union, but I hoped
" to engage my sister-in-law to be my
" advocate with her husband. The
" father of my mistress, nettled at the
" Marquis's refusal, gave me but a
" very short time to win his consent,
" and declared both to me and his
" daughter,

3

" daughter, that at the expiration of
" that time he would marry her to
" another.

" The friendſhip with which Ma-
" dam de Benavides treated me,
" prompted me to beg her aſſiſtance.
" I went often to her apartment deter-
" mined to ſpeak to her, and as often
" I ſuffered the moſt trivial circum-
" ſtance to prevent me. Mean while
" the time preſcribed expired. I had
" before received many letters from
" my miſtreſs, preſſing me to be ex-
" peditious; my anſwers, unperceived
" by me, were fraught with cold-
" neſs, which ſubjected me to her
                              " reproaches.

" reproaches. I could not but think
" them unjuſt, and told her my opi-
" nion.—She believed herſelf for-
" ſaken ; and indignation operating
" with her father's entreaties, pre-
" vailed on her to marry. She her-
" ſelf acquainted me with it. Her
" letter, though teeming with re-
" proach, was tender ; and ſhe con-
" cluded with requeſting me never
" to ſee her more. I had moſt ſin-
" cerely loved her, and believe our
" love was mutual ; I could not there-
" fore bear my loſs without unfeigned
" ſorrow. I feared ſhe was unhappy,
" and upbraided myſelf with being
" the author of her miſery.

" Theſe

" Thefe different thoughts were
" playing on my imagination as I
" was walking in the grove near the
" caftle, when I accidentally met
" Madam de Benavides. She obferved
" my uneafinefs, and kindly enquired
" the reafon. A fecret reluctance re-
" ftrained my anfwer. I could not
" prevail on myfelf to tell her I was
" in love; but the pleafure to talk
" to her of loye, though for another
" object, tempted me much. I dared
" not examine my own fentiments in
" refpect to my fifter-in-law. At
" length, after much hefitation, I men-
" tioned the caufe of my uneafinefs,
                                        " and

" and shewed her the letter of Ma-
" demoiselle de Valiere."

" Why have you thus been silent
" said she? had you mentioned it to
" me, I might perhaps have gained
" your brother's consent, though he
" gave you the denial. How much
" I pity you! how sincerely concern-
" ed am I for her! She will be most
" unhappy!" " Madam de Benavides
" compassion for the lady induced
" me to think that she had not a
" disadvantageous opinion of me.
" To lessen her concern, I told her
" that Mademoiselle's husband was a
" man of merit, of considerable rank,
" and

" and had a profpect of a princely
" fortune." " You deceive yourfelf,
" fays fhe, if you fuppofe thofe things
" can make her happy. Nothing can
" compenfate for the lofs of him we
" love. It is a dreadful thing to fub-
" ftitute duty in the place of affec-
" tion." " Frequent fighs efcaped her
" during this converfation; and her
" eyes were dim with tears.

" She faid no more, but left me.
" I could not follow her; grief had
" deprived me both of fpeech and
" motion. I could not but fee what
" I had hitherto fhut my eyes againft,
" that I was in love with my fifter. —
                    " I like-

" I likewise suspected that her heart
" was engaged to another. I re-
" collected a thousand circumstances
" which before I had not attended to.
" Her taste for solitude, her indiffe-
" rence to amusements, her exceffive
" melancholy, which I had attributed
" to my brother's usage, seemed now
" to spring from another cause. Re-
" flections the most gloomy presented
" themselves to my view. Every
" duty social and divine forbade my
" love." " Were not her affections
" engaged to another, said I, my love
" though hopeless, yet would have
" its sweets. Her friendship without
" a blush of guilt I might demand.

K   " But

" But what avails her friendſhip,
" while her heart is warmed with the
" more lively ſentiments of love ?"
" I was conſcious that I ought to
" wean myſelf of a paſſion ſo fatal
" to my repoſe and repugnant to
" my honour ; and determined to fly
" thoſe dangers, which I dared not
" meet. I returned to the caſtle to
" apprize my brother of my depar-
" ture ; but the ſight of Madam de
" Benavides obliterated my reſolu-
" tions. Yet to have ſome pretext
" to ſtay, I cheated myſelf into the
" perſuaſion, that my preſence pre-
" vented in ſome meaſure my bro-
" ther's ill uſage.

" It

" It was about that time you ar-
" rived at the caſtle. Your air and
" manner contradicted your profeſſion.
" I therefore made you a tender of
" my friendſhip, and wiſhed to ob-
" tain your confidence, as I intended
" to engage you to draw Madam de
" Benavides picture. For in defiance
" of all the illuſions of love I retained
" my purpoſe of leaving the houſe ;
" and as I intended never to return,
" I was extremely ſolicitous to carry
" with me her picture. The manner
" in which you refuſed my advances,
" told me I could have no dependance
" on you ; I therefore applied to
" another painter the very day you

K 2   had

" had that unhappy rencounter with
" my brother. Judge of my fur-
" prife, when on my return I learned
" what had paffed. My brother pre-
" ferved a gloomy filence, but darted
" looks of fury at his wife, who was
" weeping by him. As foon as I had
" entered the room, "deliver me, faid
" he, from the fight of this crocodile
" who has betrayed me, conduct
" her to her apartment, and let her
" be confined." I would have fpoken,
but he inftantly ftopped me by faying, " Obey me this moment, or
" fee my face no more."——" I was
" obliged to obey. I approached my
" fifter-in-law, and begged leave to
" fpeak

" fpeak with her in her own apart-
" ment. " Well, faid fhe, fhedding a
" flood of tears, execute your or-
" ders."———

" Thefe words, which carried with
" them the air of reproach, cut me to
" the heart. Before my brother I
" dared not reply; but as foon as I
" had waited on Madam de Benavides
" to her apartment, madam, faid I,
" with a look expreffive of the moft
" melancholy tendernefs, do you con-
" found me with your perfecutor?
" I enter into all your cares,
" and will freely lay down my life
" to ferve you. I fhudder at the
K 3 " thought,

" thought, it may be ill grounded,
" but I tremble for your life.——For
" heaven's fake fly the danger which
" awaits you, and fuffer me to con-
" duct you to a place of fafety."

" I know not that the Marquis will
" facrifice me to his vengeance ; but
" I know that it is my duty to con-
" tinue with him, and my duty I will
" fulfil, though the confequence be
" fatal. She was filent for a moment,
" then renewing her difcourfe, I am
" going, continued fhe, by my confi-
" dence, to give you the ftrongeft
" affurance of my efteem. But I
" muft, at the fame time that I pay you
" that

" that compliment, attend alfo to your
" welfare.   Return therefore to your
" brother immediately, a long con-
" verfation may beget fufpicion, but
" fee me again as foon as poffible."—

" My immediate departure was an
" inftance of my obedience. The fur-
" geon had given orders, that the Mar-
" quis fhould be left alone ; I there-
" fore inftantly returned to his lady,
" perplexed with a thoufand doubts
" and inquietudes. I wifhed to know,
" what at the fame time I was afraid
" to hear.—Madam de Benavides men-
" tioned her knowledge of you, and
" confeffed the affection which was fo
K 4   " deeply

" deeply rooted in your heart; neither
" did she dissemble her own inclinati-
" ons."—Have I then (cried I, interrupting the Chevalier) have I won
the affections of the most lovely of her
sex?—and have I lost her?——

This idea penetrated my heart with
such tender sentiments, that I melted
into tears. —" Yes, continued he, you
" were loved indeed.—Her every word
" spake tenderness, her every look af-
" fection. Her heart was wholly yours.
" I perceived, that she dwelled with
" pleasure on every circumstance of
" your behaviour. She acknowledged
" that she knew you the moment she
                                    " entered

" entered the room you was painting,
" that she had written to you, entreat-
" ing you to leave the house, but never
" had an opportunity to give it you.
" She then minutely informed me of
" the Marquis's surprising you at the
" very instant you was bidding her an
" eternal adieu; and that he would
" have sacrificed her to his fury, had
" it not been for your interposition.
" Save him, added she, save my unfor-
" tunate lover from his impending fate.
" Too well I know, that he will suffer
" the most agonizing tortures without
" confession; the rack will not extort
" from him a discovery which might
" expose me to ruin.

" Your

" Your good opinion, Madam, said
" I, is a full recompence for all his
" sufferings." "To you (replied Madam
" de Benavides) I have discovered with-
" out disguise my weakness. But re-
" member, although I have not been
" mistress of my inclinations, yet I have
" of my conduct ; and that I have not
" even been guilty of an indiscretion
" the most rigid duty could condemn."

" Alas madam, to me your justifica-
" tion is surperfluous ! that our hearts
" are not at our own disposal, is a me-
" lancholy truth, of which I am a most
" unfortunate example.——Be assured
" that I will serve you to the utmost,
" and

" and will, if poſſible, ſet the Count
" of Comminge at liberty, who (par-
" don me madam) is not perhaps the
" moſt unhappy.———

" In pronouncing theſe words I with-
" drew, not daring to lift my eyes
" from the ground. I fled to my
" own apartment, and conſidered the
" part I was to act. I determined at
" all events to deliver you ; but I was
" debating, whether I ought not like-
" wiſe to fly myſelf: for my ſufferings,
" during the recital of her misfortunes,
" convinced me of the exceſs of my
" paſſion, and I knew the neceſſity of
" weaning myſelf of an attachment ſo
                              " repugnant

" repugnant to every principle of vir-
" tue. But the cruelty of leaving Ma-
" dam de Benavides to the fury of her
" hufband, determined me after much
" wavering, to contribute by my ftay
" to her affiftance, but moft ftudioufly
" to avoid her prefence.

" I was many days without feeing
" her, but my brother's being in im-
" minent danger obliged me to wait
" on Madam de Benavides.

" If, faid fhe, I had loft the Marquis
" by the common courfe of nature, I
" fhould not have been fo fenfibly affec-
" ted. But the unhappy part I have
been

" been innocently engaged in, makes
" me infupportably wretched. I regard
" not his ill treatment, but I tremble
" at the idea of his dying with a bad
" opinion of my conduct. Should he
" furvive, I truft, my innocence will
" prevail over appearance, and that I
" again fhall enjoy, as I have merited,
" his efteem.—I muft likewife, madam,
" replied I, endeavour to obtain yours.
" I implore forgivenefs for the difco-
" very of my fentiments—fentiments
" I could neither prevent nor conceal.
" I know not that I can conquer this
" unhappy paffion, but I moft folemn-
" ly declare that I will never affront you
" more by revealing it. Had not your
" intereft

3

Can't escape misery from men

" interest detained me, I before had
" banished myself your presence. I
" confess, replied Madam de Benavi-
" des, <u>that you have added much to</u>
" <u>the measure of my misery.</u> Fate has
" deprived me of the consolation
" which I found in your friendship.

 " Her tears were more persuasive
" than all the powers of reason. I was
" ashamed to aggravate the miseries of
" one so wretched.—No, madam, you
" shall not lose that friendship you was
" so gracious as to value. My struggles
" to obliterate all traces of my error
" shall render me not wholly undeserv-
" ing your esteem.

      " I found

" I found myself on taking leave
" more tranquil, and perceived a com-
" pofure in my mind, to which I had
" been before a ftranger. So far from
" avoiding her prefence, I took every
" opportunity of being with her, that
" I might have new reafons for con-
" firming myfelf in my duty. Succefs
" fmiled on my endeavours ; and by
" degrees my paffion glided into the
" more tranquil path of friendfhip. I
" acquainted Madam de Benavides with
" the progrefs of my reformation ; fhe
" confeffed her acknowledgments, as
" for a fervice I had done her, and by
" way of recompence gave me moredif-
" tinguifhed marks of her confidence.

" My

" My heart would sometimes revolt,
" but reason kept its state.———

" My brother at length recovered;
" he had not, during his illness, suffer-
" ed his wife to see him; and before he
" left his chamber, Madam de Bena-
" vides was seized with a fever. She
" was indebted to youth for her reco-
" very; and I had reason to conclude
" that her illness would have effected a
" reconciliation.———

" Although the Marquis in the
" height of his illness had peremptorily
" refused her solicitations to see him;
" yet he now enquired after her, with
" an earnestness bordering on affection.
" She

" She was in a fair way of recovery, when the Marquis ordered me to attend him. I have fome bufinefs of confequence, faid he, which requires my prefence at Angers; my health will not fuffer me to make the journey, you will oblige me in tranfacting the bufinefs; I have ordered my fervants and equipage to attend you, and beg you will ufe all poffible expedition. I was fo much younger than my brother, that I refpected him as a parent; and as I had no reafon to excufe myfelf from the journey, I prepared for my immediate departure. But I thought this inftance of my complaifance entitled me to recommend

L   Madam

Madam de Benavides to the return of his favour. What did I not urge to mitigate his wrath! I flattered myself I had moved his pity, and that his heart relented."

" I did love Madam de Benavides, said my brother, with the pureſt affection, ſhe yet has ſtrong hold upon my heart; time and her future conduct may perhaps efface from my memory, what my eyes were ſuch melancholy witneſſes of." "I did not pretend to diſpute with him the juſtneſs of his anger. I thought it of ſome conſequence to have allayed his fury. I begged permiſſion to acquaint my

sister

another love interest

fifter with the hopes he had given me, to which he readily affented. Poor woman ! fhe heard the news with joy. I know, faid fhe, that I never can be happy with the Marquis, but it will be great confolation to conform to the dictates of my duty.———

" I took my leave, having again af-fured her of my brother's favourable fentiments. One of the domefticks, in whom I could confide, received my injunctions to be moft mi-nutely attentive to every thing which regarded his miftrefs, and to acquaint me with it. After thefe precautions, which I deemed fufficient, I took the

L 2 road

road to Angers. I had been there fifteen days without hearing from the castle. At length I received a letter from the domestick, who told me that my brother had difmissed all his fervants, except one man, whom he still retained in his fervice. This letter filled my foul with apprehenfion; without finifhing my bufinefs, I took post immediately.

" I was on my journey from thence when I received the fatal news of Madam de Benavides's death; my brother, who had written at the fame time, appeared fo affected at her lofs, that I could not believe him guilty of contri-

contributing to fo melancholy an event. He faid, that his affection had weaned him fo much from his refentment, that nothing but her fudden death prevented his abfolute forgivenefs. I have learnt fince my arrival here, that fhe relapfed foon after my departure, and expired in three days. My brother remains plunged in the deepeft melancholy, denies himfelf to every one, and begs that I will not as yet wait upon him. I obey his commands with pleafure; fince every object there would recal Madam de Benavides to my memory, and more fenfibly aggravate my forrows.

L 3   I fear

[158]

" I fear her death has revived my shameful paffion; as I know not whether love does not contribute more than friendfhip to my tears. I am fo tortured with my own melancholy reflections, that I am determined to go immediately into Hungary, where I hope, amidft the perils of war, I fhall either recover my long-loft tranquillity, or find in an honourable death a period to my woes."——

I would have thanked him for his melancholy narrative, but my voice was choaked with fighs, my eyes were dim with tears. He feemed not lefs affected; and withdrew with

Don

Don Jerome to leave me to my reflections.

The relation I had juſt heard ſpurred on my impatience to bid adieu to ſociety, and to ſecrete myſelf where melancholy reigned alone. My earneſtneſs to reduce my reſolutions into practice contributed greatly to my recovery. My ſtrength returned, my wound cloſed, and I was after ſome weeks languiſhing able to endure the fatigues of a journey. My laſt interview with Don Jerome was very affecting. His words, his looks, his wiſhes, breathed the honeſt air of friendſhip and affection. But I was

ſo

fo abforbed in the idea of Adelaid, that my heart made but an ungrateful return. I concealed my defign, leaft the officioufnefs of my friends fhould prevent my putting it in execution. I wrote to my mother by St. Laurent, whom I recommended to her protection; I gave her a minute detail of every circumftance of my misfortunes; I mentioned my refolution of fequeftering myfelf from the world, and told her, that I thought it my duty to remove from her eye, a wretch whofe only wifh was death, and that if fhe was defirous of obliging me, fhe would not attempt difcovering my retreat. I gave St. Laurent at his

2   departure

departure my all, having referved a mere fufficiency for my journey. Madam de Benavides's letter and picture, which I always carried at my heart, were the only riches I valued and retained.———

I left the convent, and came without any interruption to the Abbey of la Trappe. Immediately on my arrival I requefted the habit, which the principal of the order refufed, alledging that I muft firft go through my novitiate. I completed my trial without a murmur, and when I was afked whether the meannefs of my diet and the aufterities prefcribed were not unequal

equal to my refo'ution ; fuch had been
the power of my grief, that I anfwered,
that I was a ftranger both to the
coarfenefs of diet, and the aufterities
which they mentioned.——

My infenfibility was conftrued into
zeal, and I was immediately admitted.
The affurance that my tears could
not now be interrupted, and that my
whole life wou'd be fpent in the ex-
ercife of affliction adminiftered me
fome confolation. The folitude, the
filence of this feat of mifery, together
with the melancholy which was ftampt
on every face, contributed not a little
to the nourifhing of my grief. I
went

went through the duties of the convent without repining, for to me
every thing was equally indifferent.
I every day fecreted myfelf in the
bofom of the woods, where I red my
Adelaid's letter, and dwelt on every
word : there I examined her picture,
till imagination gave it life; I bathed
both the one and the other with my
tears, and returned to the convent
more ineffably miferable.

In this manner had I lingered on
for three long years, a life of mifery
without the leaft alloy, when the
bell fummoned me to affift at the
laft moments of a brother. He

was

was lying on a plank ftrewed with afhes and receiving the extreme unction, when he begged permiffion to break filence.———

"What I fhall fay my father (ad-
"dreffing himfelf to the principal of
"our fociety) will animate my au-
"ditors with new fervour towards
"the Almighty; who by ways the
"moft extraordinary, has fnatched
"me from a gulph of mifery to fteer
"me into the harbour of eternal fal-
"vation."———

He thus proceeded,———

"I dif-

" I difgrace the name of brother,
" with which thefe holy men have
" honoured me. In me, behold—
" a wretched, finful woman. Whom
" love, unholy love, conducted hi-
" ther.——I loved and was beloved
" by a man of equal rank. But
" the animofity of our parents
" was a fatal obftacle to our union,
" and I was obliged for the welfare of
" my lover to give my hand a rebel
" to my heart. Even in the choice
" of a hufband, I fought only to give
" a proof of the extravagance of my
" paffion: and he who could infpire
" hate alone, was to obviate my
" lover's jealoufy, to all unworthily
                              " pre-

" preferred. But it was the will of
" the Almighty, that a marriage thus
" contracted with views so criminal,
" should be to me an uninterrupted
" source of misery. Behold! my
" husband and my lover, by each
" other wounded, bleeding before
" my eyes! A scene so shocking threw
" me into a fever; from which I was
" scarce recovered, when my husband
" immured me in a dungeon, and
" made report declare me dead. In
" this place of horror I lingered out
" two years, to every consolation alike
" a stranger. My husband, unsated
" with my sufferings, had the cruelty
" to add insult to misery. What do
" I say ?

" I fay?——My God! dare I brand
" with cruelty the inftrument you
" thought meet to be my punifhment!
" My miferies, heavy as they were,
" opened not my eyes to my errors ;
" when I fhould have wept my fins,
" I could only lament my lover.——
" The death of my hufband at length
" procured my liberty.——The do-
" meftick who alone was confcious of
" my fate, opened my prifon ; but at
" the fame time informed me, that
" I had been reputed dead from the
" firft moment of my confinement.

" The noife my adventure would
" occafion, determined me on retire-
" ment ;

" ment; a refolution I the more
" readily embraced, as all my in-
" quiries were fruitlefs after the only
" perfon for whom I wifhed to live.
" That I might the more eafily fteal
" unnoticed from the caftle, I dif-
" guifed myfelf in the habit of a
" man, in which I purpofed travelling
" to a convent in the neighbourhood
" of Paris. I was haftening thither,
" when a fecret impulfe, as I paffed
" this feat of religion, obliged me
" to enter your chapel. On the inftant
" of my entrance I diftinguifhed in
" the fulnefs of the anthem, a voice
" too well accuftomed to fink into
" my heart. I believed myfelf fe-
" duced

" duced by the powers of imagina-
" tion. — I drew near, and through all
" the changes which time and auste-
" rities had made on his countenance,
" I recognized the man so dear to
" my memory. My God! how vio-
" lent were my agitations! how im-
" pious were my thoughts! I dared
" blaspheme the author of my being
" for seducing my lover from me.
" You punished not my impious
" murmurs, O my God! but made
" my miseries promote my eternal
" welfare. I could not force myself
" from the place, which held my
" very soul. And that I no more
" might lose him, I offered myself to

M   " you

" you my father for the habit. With
" such earneſtneſs I prayed admit-
" tance, that you admitted me. How
" did I perform your holy exerciſe!
" A heart throbbing with guilty paſ-
" ſion, my ſoul wrapped up in him I
" loved.

" The Almighty by abandoning me
" to myſelf, was willing to give me
" more powerful reaſons for my fu-
" ture humiliation. He therefore
" ſuffered me to taſte the empoiſoned
" joys of breathing the ſame air, and
" of being under the ſame roof with
" him, who innocently had ſeduced
" my ſoul from his holy preſence.

" I

" I haunted my lover as his shadow,
" I assisted his labours with all my
" little strength, and in those mo-
" ments was amply paid my every
" trouble. My infatuation would
" have led me to discover myself,
" had I not been restrained by the
" dread of interrupting the tran-
" quillity of him, who had robbed
" me of my repose. Yes—thou be-
" nevolent author of my being, I
" should have endeavoured to seduce
" that soul which I believed wholly
" thine !—

" At the expiration of two months
" each man was obliged to dig his
M 2 " grave,

" grave, agreeable to the founder's
" inftitution, who by a perpetual
" idea of death intended to render
" holy the lives of his order.

" I attended as ufual on him to
" whom I was bound by chains fo
" fhameful. The fight of his grave,
" and the zeal with which he dug it,
" penetrated my heart with fuch a
" lively forrow, that to conceal my
" weaknefs I was obliged to retire.
" It feemed the very moment in
" which I fhould for ever lofe him.
" This idea preyed on my imagina-
" tion, and if I left him but a few
" hours,

" hours, I feared I should never see
" him more.

" Behold the happy moment
" which God had prepared to win me
" to himself!——We were cutting
" wood in the forest for the supply
" of the convent.—My lover had
" unperceived escaped from me. My
" solicitude prompted me to search
" for him through all the mazes of
" the wood; at last I espied him in
" a part the most retired, poring
" over some thing which hung at his
" bosom. His attention was so ab-
" sorbed, that I drew near unnoticed,
" and surveyed the object of his con-

M 3   " templation.

" templation. How inexpreffible was
" my amazement at feeing my own
" picture. Then I perceived, that
" fo far from enjoying the repofe I
" dreaded to difturb, that he was like
" myfelf, an unhappy victim to a
" more unhappy paffion.—Then did
" my imagination paint the Almighty
" in his anger ready to lay his heavy
" hand upon him. I trembled leaft
" the love which I had impioufly
" carried with me to his holy altar,
" fhould draw down the vengeance
" of heaven on the unhappy object
" of it. Full of this idea, I proftrated
" myfelf before his holy fhrine. I
" prayed for my converfion, that I
                              " might

2

" might obtain it for my lover.—Yes
" my God, it was for him alone I
" offered you my prayers. It was
" for him alone my tears were fhed.
" It was my anxiety for his happinefs,
" which made me a profelyte to
" righteoufnefs.—You looked down
" with an eye of mercy on my weak-
" nefs. My prayers all infufficient,
" all impious as they were, were
" not rejected. An emanation of
" your holy grace defcended into my
" heart. Then did I tafte that peace
" of mind, which fouls dedicated to
" thy fervice can alone enjoy.———

" You

" You willed by my fufferings to
" add yet more to my purification.——
" But hold.——I feel the hand of
" death upon me.——If the com-
" panion of my infatuation ftill la-
" bours under the oppreffion of ini-
" quity, let him reflect on the ob-
" ject of his foolifh paffion, let him
" caft his eye on me ; let him think
" on that tremendous moment which
" now awaits me, and which he foon
" muft know.   The period of my
" exiftence is arrived ; I implore the
" prayers of thefe holy men ; I requeft
" their pardon for the offence I have
" given, and I acknowledge myfelf
                              " unworthy

She dies, ~~somet~~ tragic.

" unworthy to partake of their fe-
" pulture."————

Language cannot paint the feelings
of my foul; I experienced in that
tremendous moment all the tendernefs
of love and agonizing horrors of defpair. I was kneeling with the other
religious, when firft fhe fpake; the
voice I inftantly knew to be the
voice of Adelaid; but the fear of
lofing a fingle word fhe uttered, reftrained my cries. When I found
fhe was expired, I grew delirious with
grief; I fprung from the religious
who had crowded to my affiftance;
I threw myfelf on my knees, I feized
her

her lifeleſs hand and bathed it with a torrent of tears.——" Now I have for " ever loſt you; my deareſt Adelaid " was with me, and my heart un- " grateful knew her not.——No— " we will part no more.——Death " leſs cruel than my father, ſhall " unite us now for ever."———

My holy brethren melted at this ſpectacle of woe, endeavoured by the moſt pathetic and chriſtian exhorta- tions to remove me from the body, which I held in my embrace. Force ſucceeded to entreaties, and I was confined in my cell.

The

The father Abbot attended me the whole night, and endeavoured to mitigate my forrows, but he could not win on my affliction.

" Reftore me Adelaid, faid I, why
" have you feparated us? No—I can-
" not, will not live where fhe fo much
" has fuffered. For pity's fake per-
" mit me to quit this place! What
" would you with a wretch like me.
" My defpair will poifon that tran-
" quillity, which has ever flourifhed
" here. Suffer me to retire to fome
" fequeftered vale far from the haunts
" of men. My Adelaid will inter-
" cede with the Almighty for a re-
                              " miffion

" miffion of my fins.——And you,
" my father, be propitious to this
" my laft requeft. Promife me, that
" the fame tomb fhall unite our afhes,
" there we may fleep in peace.——I
" in return moft folemnly proteft,
" that I will not expedite that hour,
" which can alone remove my
" cares."————

The father Abbot foftened into
pity, and willing probably to remove from the eye of his convent
an object fo difgraceful, yielded to
my preffing importunities.

I in-

I inſtantly bade adieu to the Abbey of la Trappe, and came to this hermitage, where I have ſpent many years in no other employ, than in bewailing with tears my loſs.———

F I N I S.

TRAVELLING.

This day is Published,

In One Vol. Price 3s.

With a correct Map of all the Post and Crofs
Roads, Towns, and Villages,

THE GENTLEMAN's GUIDE
in his Tour through FRANCE.

By an OFFICER.

Containing an accurate Defcription of that
Country. Including Paris, Verfailles, Fonten-
bleau, Morley, St. Germains, St. Cloud, and
every Public Building and Place worthy a Tra-
veller's Notice. Lifts of Lodging-houfes, Or-
dinaries, Places of Amufement, with their Prices;
Stage-Coaches and Water Carriages to different
Parts of the Kingdom, with their Fares; and
every other Particular neceffary for the Information of Strangers.

Printed for G. Kearfly, No. 46, Fleet-ftreet,
and G. Robinfon, Paternofter-row.

Of whom may be had,

The Tour of Holland, Dutch Barbant, the Auſtrian Netherlands, and Part of France; in which is included, a Deſcription of Paris and its Environs.

Alſo, USEFUL HINTS to thoſe who make the Tour of France. In a Series of Letters written from that Kingdom.

By PHILIP THICKNESSE, Eſq.

Theſe Letters (none of which were ever pnbliſhed before) contain ſome Account of the Interior Police in general, and of Paris in particular. With a conſiderable Number of entertaining Anecdotes, relative to the firſt Perſoaages on that Part of the Continent.

☞ Theſe Three Volumes, which may be had ſeparate or together, Price 3s. each, will enable Travellers to make the Tour of France and the low Countries; as they contain every Thing worthy the Attention of the moſt minute Enquirer; and will prevent, if properly attended to, the ſcandalous Impoſitions too often practiced by the Publicans upon the Continent.

The laſt Article only is written by Mr. Thickneſſe.

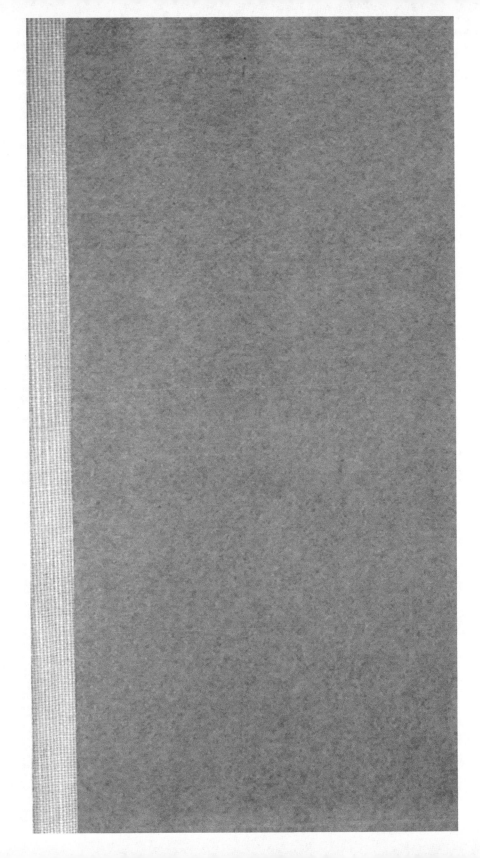

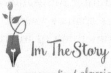

WS - #0021 - 180124 - C0 - 229/152/12 - PB - 9780371916575 - Gloss Lamination